The Chaplet
of Reparation
AND OTHER PRAYERS
from

IN SINU JESU

with

THE EPIPHANY
CONFERENCE
of
Mother Mectilde de Bar

ANGELICO PRESS

First published in the USA
by Angelico Press 2018
Copyright © Angelico Press 2018

For information, address:
Angelico Press, Ltd.
169 Monitor St.
Brooklyn, NY 11222
www.angelicopress.com

978-1-62138-347-5 (paper)

Book and cover design
by Michael Schrauzer

CONTENTS

FOREWORD

READERS OF *IN SINU JESU* HAVE asked if the prayers—especially the Chaplet of Reparation—might be made available as a separate publication. The result is the present little book, which contains all the prayers scattered throughout *In Sinu Jesu* and collected in that book's first Appendix, while also adding a translation by a Benedictine monk of a conference given on Epiphany in 1694 by Mother Mectilde de Bar (1614–1698), foundress of the Benedictines of Perpetual Adoration of the Most Blessed Sacrament. *In Sinu Jesu* refers to this great spiritual figure several times (see pp. 176, 190–94, 212, 234, 242, 259).

May these fervent prayers and this marvelous conference generate light and warmth in the souls of all who take them up, especially in the privileged moments of Eucharistic adoration.

A Benedictine Oblate

INTRODUCTION
to the Epiphany Conference
by
A Benedictine Monk

OTHER MECTILDE DE BAR gave one of her most important conferences on the vigil of the Epiphany, 1694. She would have been eighty years old at the time; this conference reflects, then, her thought in its maturity. The message of Mother Mectilde de Bar speaks to the heart of anyone called by God to a life of adoration.

Mother Mectilde affirms, first of all, that the Most Holy Eucharist contains all the mysteries of Christ or, if you will, Christ in all His mysteries. The mysteries of Christ are theandric events: they correspond to Christ's twofold nature, divine and human. Insofar as they are human, the events of Christ's life are subject to the passing flow of time in history; they took place at a given moment in a given place. Insofar as they are divine, these same events transcend time and space, remaining ever present and actual in the Most Holy Sacrament of the Altar. The mystery-events of Christ contained in the Most Holy Eucharist are eternally present to the Father and, in time, are perpetually available to the Church, to whom it is given to apply their fruits sacramentally for the forgiveness of sins and for the growth in holiness of the faithful.

Mother Mectilde's theological thought is strongly related to her experience of the sacred liturgy and, notably, to the Holy Sacrifice of the Mass. One detects in this conference resonances of the Preface of the Mass and of the Sanctus. Mother Mectilde relates the grandeur of the heavenly liturgy in all its perfection to the vocation of those whom God has chosen to adore Him in spirit and in truth here below.

Mother Mectilde further relates adoration to the immolation of the victim made over to God in sacrifice. Sacrifice is, in fact, the supreme expression of adoration. One cannot adore in spirit and in truth while witholding something of oneself from God. One's whole self must be surrendered in a sacrificial holocaust in order for one's adoration to be what God would have it be. For this reason did the Father give us the sacrifice of the Son—the pure Victim, the holy

Victim, the spotless Victim (as the Roman Canon puts it) — as the pattern of adoration to be reproduced in all who belong to Him, and this by the power of the Holy Spirit.

Spontaneously, Mother Mectilde breaks into prayer in the middle of her conference. In this she follows a long monastic tradition, exemplified notably by Saint Bernard, in which the speaker quite naturally addresses God, even while addressing men.

There is an almost humourous realism in Mother Mectilde's comparison of one attempting to adore God worthily with the buzzing flight of little flies who can only go so high without falling exhausted to the ground. (Anyone who has had to sweep up dead flies from a window ledge or elsewhere, knows exactly what she is talking about.) Adoration in spirit and in truth is, before all else, a grace that God gives us before being something that we can give God.

One of the most remarkable characteristics of Mother Mectilde's teaching is her conviction that all of the baptized are called to holiness. This is borne out in her rich correspondence with laymen and laywomen living in the world. She never hesitates to invite them to the same life of victimhood through Jesus, with Jesus, and in Jesus that she presents to her daughters in so compelling a way. The life of perpetual adoration is not for a coterie of elite souls; it belongs to the life of all who, being baptized, are called to become the adorers in spirit and in truth whom the Father seeks.

Mother Mectilde's teaching corresponds to that of Saint Paul: "Whatever you are about, in word and action alike, invoke always the name of the Lord Jesus Christ, offering your thanks to God the Father through him" (Colossians 3:17). Mother Mectilde's insistence on the victimal character of the Christian life is a uncompromising and wholehearted response to Saint Paul's injunction to the Romans: "And now, brethren, I appeal to you by God's mercies to offer up your bodies as a living sacrifice, consecrated to God and worthy of his acceptance; this is the worship due from you as rational creatures" (Romans 12:1).

A life of adoration here below is a foretaste of heaven. One who adores perpetually in this life, who adores with every breath and every heart-beat, is doing already what he will do eternally in heaven. Here one adores in the darkness of faith; there it will be in the light of glory.

4

In conclusion, Mother Mectilde wisely counsels against seeking extraordinary sensible manifestations of God's will, subject to illusion and to deception. Instead, she invites her hearers to incline the ear of their heart to the quiet inward inspiration of the Holy Spirit and to respond to the voice of Christ who, speaking in silence, says, "Adore Me in spirit and in truth."

THE EPIPHANY CONFERENCE

OMORROW WE SHALL celebrate the feast of the Epiphany, which signifies the manifestation of Jesus to the holy Magi Kings, who sought Him in the manger of Bethlehem to offer Him their respect and their adoration. This feast must bring us a special devotion because it corresponds more than any other to the spirit of our vocation which deputes us to adore the same Christ Jesus, whom the Magi adored, in the august Sacrament of the Altar, the mystery that contains within itself all the other mysteries of His holy life. For this reason, you can adore there [in the Most Holy Sacrament] the little Child of the manger; you can adore Him together with the Holy Kings and you can say even as they did, "We have seen his star in the east, and are come to adore him" (Matthew 2:2). The call to the Institute [of Perpetual Adoration of the Most Holy Sacrament of the Altar] was your star, and even though you did not see a visible star, as the Magi did, you have had nonetheless the interior inspiration of grace, which is by far more secure than outward signs.

You have, then, seen His star, and you have come to adore Him. But what duration and extent must such adoration have? Every instant of our life, and with all our being. We are called...of Perpetual Adoration. Oh, let us not bear so beautiful a name in vain; let us not be illusory adorers, let us correspond with all our capacity to this calling and to God's choice of us to adore Him continually. Has He need of us for this, poor and miserable creatures that we are who can do nothing good of ourselves unless we be moved by His grace? Has He not millions of angels and heavenly spirits who ceaselessly render Him perfect adoration even in our churches, which are altogether full of them? Although we do not see them, this is the truth. All the same, He has chosen us and wants us to have the privilege of adoring Him as they do, and of being His perpetual adorers. We must, in a holy manner, glory in so lofty a vocation! But to carry out such a vocation, it is not enough to spend an hour or some in His presence in choir.[1]

---

1   In a monastic church the "choir" is the space set apart for the celebration of the Divine Office and for adoration of the Most Blessed Sacrament by the monks or nuns.

Our adoration must be perpetual because the same God whom we adore in the Most Holy Sacrament is always present to us in every place. We must adore Him in spirit and in truth.[2] In spirit, by means of a holy interior recollection; in truth, by acting in such wise that all our observances become a continual adoration, and this by giving ourselves faithfully to God in all that He asks of us, because as soon as we fail in fidelity, we stop adoring.

Our Institute was created uniquely to make perpetual adorers of us. You have been called to this; it is, therefore, up to you to realise its grace and holiness by becoming authentic adorers who adore in spirit and in truth. Yes, such must be your care and diligence in adoring this God of majesty in spirit and in truth, so as to correspond to His choice of you. In spirit, by the certainty of your faith, believing all that He is in Himself, even without understanding it. His divine greatnesses and perfections deserve your homage, your respect, your adoration. In truth, by adoring Him with your whole being, in such wise that there be nothing in you that you do not wish to hand over and sacrifice to Him in order to adore Him as perfectly

---

2 John 4:24.

as possible according to your capacity and with all your heart.

My God, what an honour Thou hast done us in calling us to adore Thee! Grant us the grace to correspond to this calling. We ask this of Thee through the mediation of Thy most holy Mother, even as we pray her to obtain for us from Thy bounty that we may know how to fulfil faithfully the obligation of adoring Thee — adoring Thee in spirit and in truth — with our entire selves, immolating to Thy greatness all that we are.

I repeat it to you again, let us consider well the grace that the Lord has bestowed on us: He has chosen us to adore Him always, we who barely know how to think of Him and who are like poor little flies in His presence! When we think that we are lifting ourselves up a little to God in contemplation, we fall down right away. The distraction of our spirit and of our imagination, our darknesses, our personal miseries are so great! No matter how much good will we may have, it is impossible for us to maintain always our mind equally raised up to God. Our adorations on earth are but momentary, so to speak, in comparison with the adoration that the angels and the blessed offer God in heaven.

Why then, my God, hast Thou chosen us, poor miserable creatures? Art Thou not content with the many holy and perfect adorations that Thou receivest from the angels and saints? And if Thou hadst not enough of these, couldst Thou not create again an infinity of others similar to those whom Thou hast already created, and who would offer Thee adorations worthy of Thy divine majesty? No, my God, Thou didst will that we should share with them the honour of adoring Thee continually, beginning in this world what we will do for all eternity.

Oh, once again, how great is this grace! I assure you that only in eternity will you know its greatness! Do not think that I am telling you so many trifles to distract and entertain you. No, no, this is about certain truths that you will know after death. This is about truths of faith: according to the Gospel, God must have adorers who will adore Him in spirit and in truth.[3] It is just as certain that such is your particular vocation. And if it is your vocation, it is also a matter of faith that God has given you the grace for it. It depends, therefore, only on us to make use of it by means of our fidelity.

3   John 4:23.

To adore continually it is not necessary to say, "My God, I adore Thee." It is enough to tend inwardly to God [who is] present, to maintain a profound respect out of reverence for His greatness, believing that He is in us as He truly is. In fact, the Most Holy Trinity dwells in us: the Father acts and operates there with His power, the Son with His wisdom, and the Holy Spirit with His goodness. It is, therefore, in the intimacy of your soul, where the God of majesty abides, that you must adore Him continually.

From time to time, place your hand over your heart, saying to yourself: "God is in me. And He is there not only to sustain my physical life, as in irrational creatures, but He is there acting and operating, to raise me to the highest perfection, if I do not put obstacles in the way of His grace."

Imagine that He says to you interiorly: "I am always in thee: abide thou in Me, think of Me and I shall think of thee, and I will take care of all the rest. Be wholly at My disposal, even as I am at thine; live not apart from Me." As Scripture says, "He who eats of Me will live by Me; He will abide in Me, and I in him."[4]

---

4 John 6:58 and 6:57.

Happy are those who understand these words and who adore in spirit and in truth the Father, and the Son, and the Holy Spirit! If you wish that we return to the mystery of the Epiphany, happy too are those who adore the Child Jesus in His sacred birth, together with the holy Magi.

These holy Kings followed, then, the star that was guiding them to go in search of Jesus to adore Him. They go to Jerusalem where Herod was. He, having learned of their design, feigned that he wanted to adore Him, but this was only to take His life and do away with Him.

This, dear ones, is what befalls us every day inwardly. Our self-love is that Herod who looks only to his own interests and not to those of Jesus Christ. Often he feigns wanting to adore Him but, at bottom, He is bent only on destroying His reign and on suffocating the movements of His grace, pushing us at every turn to cling to our passions and to satisfy our senses.

We could continue to consider in the same way all that follows in this mystery, but this would take us too far afield; we would need two hours to speak to you of this, and we haven't the time. I shall, therefore, stop here, to turn back to telling you that you must be, by your profession and vocation, true and perpetual adorers of Jesus Christ. You must apply yourselves to this, and to this employ your zeal. Your most ardent desire must be that of carrying out perfectly this work of adorers.

One or another of you may say to me, "I do not quite feel this great zeal. In no way do I have the feeling of this ardent love that compels me to adore Jesus Christ in the way that you have explained." That doesn't matter; it is enough to act by faith, offering Jesus Christ your reverence and your homage. Feelings and consolations are not really necessary; on the contrary, your adoration will be purer and more perfect because the soul who has a living faith and not a sentimental one will rise more purely to God, drawn on, apart from the human senses, to what God is in Himself, in His greatness, holiness, and excellence. Do not then tarry over what your senses allow you to feel and relish; dwell, rather, on that to which faith obliges you, and on what faith makes you believe. Follow this faith, which is light to illumine you and bring you to the knowledge of this God who, with an infinite love, has called you to adore Him ceaselessly.

God has bestowed this grace upon you, pre-ferring you to so many other holy souls who are more worthy than you and who would carry out this duty better if Our Lord would show them the mercy that He has granted you, and if they were to hear His voice say to them: "Come ye to adore me. Come ye to be my perpetual adorers." How they would run [to Him]! And you also, if you were to hear these words, would you not all be transported out of yourselves for sheer joy? And even so, He has spoken these words to you in the depths of your heart, by means of the appeal of His grace, more really than if you had heard them by means of a voice's distinct sound, which could be subject to illusion and to deception. Instead, the movement of His grace and the inspiration of His Spirit within you, by which you have been called to the vocation in which you find yourselves, should give you the assurance that He has spoken these words, and that day after day He repeats them, saying to you at every moment, "Adore Me in spirit and in truth."

Oh, what a boon God has given us in choosing us! I shall never be able to repeat it enough. Our hearts must remain immersed in a continual thanksgiving towards this God of goodness. All our care must be to please Him, to serve Him, and to satisfy Him. Given that we owe Him all our very selves, is it not then just that we should give ourselves to Him, continuing faithfully to free ourselves of ourselves and of creatures, so as to devote ourselves to Him alone? This is our obligation, this is the perfection to which God calls us. But, for your consolation, I want to say to you that if you have not yet attained this perfection, it is enough that you should tend to it with all your heart. We are not, in fact, bound to be perfect all at once, but — under pain of mortal sin — we are bound to tend to perfection. Indeed, some theologians think this of all Christians. If this is so, how few will be those who are saved, given that so few think of this! But let us reflect upon ourselves since we are doubly bound to this by our profession. Let us, then, work seriously to become faithful to what we have promised to God. It is up to us to think on these things and to examine ourselves in consequence.

Oh, let us begin seriously to adore Jesus Christ in spirit and in truth, to be true perpetual adorers. Let us adore Him in all places and in all that we do. There is not a single action that can dispense us from this. You will say to me, "What, then, even while eating?" Yes, because you do not eat as animals do, only to satisfy yourselves but, rather, by way of homage and submission to the will of God, to renew your necessary strength and to sacrifice yourselves anew to His majesty. Doing this with these intentions, sanctify this action and others like it that, of themselves, are merely natural. In this way, you will maintain in these [actions] that spirit of adoration that, if you are faithful, will lead you on to the highest holiness, moving you to the perpetual sacrifice of yourselves. This will cause you to die to your passions, to your disordered inclinations and to all that is opposed to your sanctification, making you, at the same time, true victims, ever immolated to His glory and to His honour.

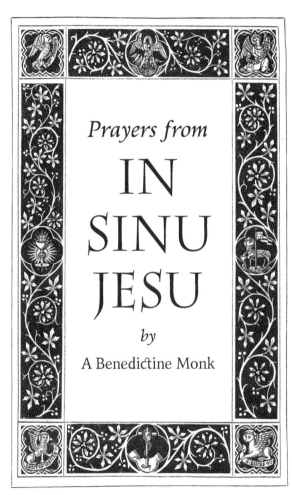

Prayers from

IN
SINU
JESU

by

A Benedictine Monk

THE CHAPLET OF
REPARATION

or,

Offering of the Precious Blood for Priests

*This chaplet of reparation and intercession
is meant to be prayed on an
ordinary five-decade rosary.*

NCLINE ✠ UNTO MY AID, O GOD; O Lord, make haste to help me. Glory be to the Father, and to the Son, and to the Holy Spirit: as it was in the beginning, is now, and ever shall be, world without end. Amen. Alleluia. (*After Septuagesima*: Praise be to Thee, O Lord, King of eternal glory.)

On the Our Father beads:

Eternal Father, I offer Thee the Precious Blood of Thy Beloved Son, our Lord Jesus Christ, the Lamb without blemish or spot, in reparation for my sins and for the sins of all Thy priests.

On the Hail Mary beads:

By Thy Precious Blood, O Jesus, purify and sanctify Thy priests.

In place of the Glory be to the Father:

O Father, from whom all fatherhood in heaven and on earth is named, have mercy on all Thy priests, and wash them in the Blood of the Lamb.

REGINA SACRATISSIMI ROSARII, ORA PRO NOBIS

VIRGIN MARY,
my Mother of Perpetual Help,
my hands are in thy hands,
and my heart is in thy heart,
and this forever.

SWEET VIRGIN MARY,
I am thy child.
Keep my hands in thy hands
and my heart in thy heart
all throughout this day
     and even during the night.
So do I want to live and die.
Amen.

MY JESUS,
I place myself in spirit
before Thy Eucharistic Face
to adore Thee,
to make reparation,
to say to Thee all that Thy Spirit of Love
    will cause to rise in my heart.
I come to look at Thee.
I come to listen to Thee.
I come to receive from Thee
    all that Thy open Heart
    desires to say to me and to give me today.
I thank Thee for having made Thyself close to me.
I praise Thy mercy.
I confess the redeeming power
    of Thy Precious Blood.
Amen.

SUMUNT BONI, SUMUNT MALI: SORTE TAMEN

INAEQUÁLI, VITAE VEL INTÉRITUS.

Y JESUS, ONLY AS THOU WILLEST,
when Thou willest,
and in the way Thou willest.
To Thee be all glory and thanksgiving,
Who rulest all things mightily and sweetly,
and Who fillest the earth
with Thy manifold mercies.
Amen.

JESUS,
I want to go in spirit
to the tabernacle
where Thou art most forsaken
and most forgotten in the world.
I want to go where no one adores Thee,
where no one bows before Thee,
where Thou hast only Thy Angels
to adore Thee and to keep Thee company.
And still, it is a human heart
that Thou desirest,
and above all, the heart of a priest.
I give Thee mine
in an offering of adoration
and reparation.

+ Introibo ad altare Dei :x: Ad Deum qui laetificat juventutem meam

ORD JESUS,
I present myself
before Thy Eucharistic Face today,
placing myself in spirit close
to that tabernacle in the world,
where Thou art most forsaken,
most ignored, and most forgotten.
Since Thou hast asked me for it,
I offer Thee my heart, the heart of a priest,
to keep company with Thy priestly and
    Eucharistic Sacred Heart.
I adore Thee in a spirit of reparation
    for all the priests of the Church,

but especially for those who never,
or hardly ever,
stop in Thy presence,
there to put down their burdens,
and to receive from Thee
 new strength,
 new lights,
 new capacities to love,
 to pardon,
 and to bless.
I do not want to leave this tabernacle today.
I want, at every instant, to remain
 immersed in the adoration for which
 Thou waitest from Thy priests.

I unite myself to the most holy Virgin Mary,
Mediatrix of all graces and first adorer
 of Thy Eucharistic Face.
By her most pure Heart,
may the prayers that rise from my heart
 reach Thy open Heart,
hidden and, so often, left alone
 in the great Sacrament of Thy love.
Amen.

MY BELOVED JESUS,
I suffer that I cannot abide
close to Thy tabernacle.
I feel deprived of Thy real presence
and, nonetheless, I rejoice
because this shows me well
how much Thou hast attached me
to the adorable Mystery
of Thy Body and Blood.
Thou willest that I should be
a priest adorer and reparator
for Thy Eucharistic Heart,
an adorer of Thy Face that,
through the Host,
shines for us.
Let this be done according to
all the desires of Thy Heart.
Amen.

Gratias agens fregit et dixit : accipite et manducate.

MY BELOVED JESUS,
the efficacy and fruitfulness
of this time of adoration
comes not from me
but from Thee.
It is all Thy doing.
I place myself before Thee
as a vessel to be filled.

MY BELOVED
and ever-merciful Jesus,
I adore Thee and I offer Thee
all the love and desire of my heart.
The desire I offer Thee is the very one
    Thou Thyself hast given me:
the desire for holiness, that is,
for union with Thee.
Unite me to Thyself:
my heart to Thy Heart,
my soul to Thy Soul,
all that I am to all that Thou art.

STRENGTHEN
my loving attention to Thee,
Thou who art lovingly attentive to me
in this the Sacrament of Thy love.

MY BELOVED JESUS,
I come before Thy Eucharistic Face
and I draw near to Thy open Heart
in this the Sacrament of Thy love,
to respond today to what Thou hast asked of me.
With trust in Thy infinite goodness,
and fearing nothing apart from sin
and the peril of separation from Thee,
I say "yes" to all that Thy Sacred Heart
desireth for me.
I want for myself only what Thou wantest for me.
I desire what Thou desirest for my life,
and nothing else.
Making use of the free will
that Thou hast given me,
I give Thee,
my Sovereign and all-powerful God,
the freedom to sanctify me wholly
in body, mind, and spirit.
I allow Thee,
as of this feast of Thy Sacred Heart,
to fashion and wound me
into a living representation of Thyself
before Thy Father and in the midst
of Thy Church.

Wound me, that I may be another Thyself
    at the altar of Thy sacrifice.
Wound me with that love that is
    indescribable in earthly terms
    so as to heal all the wounds of my sins.
Penetrate my soul with Thy divine light.
Let no vestige of darkness remain within me.
I renew my total consecration
    to the pure and sinless Heart
    of Thy Immaculate Mother,
and await from her maternal hands
    all that Thou willest to bestow upon me.
I thank Thee for Thy Mother's
    incomparable work
    in my soul and in the souls
    of all Thy priests.
Through her, I am entirely Thine.
Accomplish all the designs
    of Thy Sacred Heart upon my life.
Glory be to Thy Eucharistic Heart
    from my own heart
    and from the heart of every priest of Thine.
Amen.

 Y BELOVED JESUS,
I thank Thee for having called me
to a life of adoration.
I thank Thee
    that Thou wantest Me,
unworthy as I am,
to abide before Thy Eucharistic Face
    and to approach Thy open Heart
    in the Sacrament of Thy love.
I thank Thee that Thou hast called me
    to offer Thee reparation,
first of all for my own sins,
too many to be counted,
and for all those offences
    by which I have grieved
    Thy most loving Heart
    and offended souls dear to Thee
    and purchased by Thy most precious Blood.
Thou callest me also to make reparation
    for all the sins of my brother priests,
poor sinners like me,
often caught in the snares of the Evil One,

and insensible to the delights and peace
    that Thou desirest to give them
    in Thy presence.
I thank Thee that Thou hast chosen me
    to make reparation
    for the coldness, indifference, irreverence,
    and isolation
that Thou receivest in the Sacrament of Thy love.
To Thy presence, let me offer my presence;
to Thy pierced Heart, let me offer my heart;
to Thy divine friendship,
let me offer all the yearnings of My soul
    for that companionship of Thine,
which surpasses every passing earthly love
    and satisfies the deepest needs
    and desires of my heart.

38

BEG THEE TO KEEP ME
pure, transparent, humble, and free,
that I may fulfil with integrity,
detachment, and joy
the spiritual paternity to which Thou hast called me.
I ask moreover for the grace to relate
    to all who will come to me
    as a father to a son, as a brother to a brother.
I beg Thee to purify and strengthen
    every bond of friendship
    in the fire of Thy Eucharistic Heart.
I surrender to Thee my humanity
    with its wounds, its brokenness, and its scars.
I give Thee my past in its entirety.
I beg Thee for the grace to walk
    in the newness of life
    that I know Thou desirest for me.
And that all of this may come to pass
    in the most efficacious and fruitful way,
I abandon into the most pure hands
    of Thy Mother, my Mother,
all that I am, all that I have been, and all that Thou,
in the boundless mercy of Thy Eucharistic Heart,
wouldst have me be for Thee, O my beloved Jesus,
for Thy Mystical Body, Thy Bride, the Church,
and for the glory of Thy Father. *Amen.*

ORD JESUS CHRIST,
Priest and Victim,
Lamb without stain or blemish,
I come before Thy Face,
laden with the sins and betrayals
    of my brother priests,
and with the burden of my own sins
    and infidelities.
Allow me to represent those priests
    who are most in need of Thy mercy.
For them, let me abide before
    Thy Eucharistic Face,
close to Thy open Heart.
Through the Sorrowful and Immaculate
    Heart of Thy Mother,
Advocate and Mediatrix of all graces,
pour forth upon all the priests of Thy Church
    that torrent of mercy that ever flows
    from Thy Heart,
to purify and heal them,
to sanctify and refresh them,
and, at the hour of their death,
to make them worthy of joining Thee
    before the Father
    in the heavenly Holy Place beyond the veil.
Amen.

 MY BELOVED JESUS,
I surrender to Thy Sacred Heart
all that I love.

O THOU IN ME
and through me,
O my beloved Jesus,
all that Thou desirest to find in me
and do through me,
so that, in spite of my miseries, my weaknesses,
and even my sins,
my priesthood may be a radiance of Thine,
and my face reflect the merciful love
that ever shines on Thy Holy Face
for souls who trust in Thee
and abandon themselves
to Thy divine action.

Y JESUS,
how can I refuse Thee anything?
All my trust is in Thee.
In Thee is all my hope.
I am all Thine,
and Thy friendship is my assurance
of happiness and of Thy unfailing grace.
I give Thee my heartfelt "yes."
I am all Thine, beloved Jesus:
a priest in Thine own priesthood,
and a victim with Thee in Thy pure, holy,
and spotless oblation to the Father. *Amen.*

O MY BELOVED JESUS,
unite me to Thyself,
my body to Thy Body,
my blood to Thy Blood,
my soul to Thy Soul,
my heart to Thy Heart,
all that I am to all that Thou art:
so as to make Me with Thyself, O Jesus,
one priest and one victim
    offered to the glory of Thy Father,
out of love for Thy spouse, the Church—
for the sanctification of Thy priests,
the conversion of sinners,
the intentions of the Pope,
and in sorrowful reparation
    for my innumerable sins
    against Thee in Thy priesthood
    and in the Sacrament of Thy love.
Amen.

Y BELOVED JESUS,
I surrender to Thy Heart's love for me,
and I offer myself to Thee
as a victim of adoration
and reparation
for all whom I have hurt or offended,
that they may be healed and restored
to Thy friendship within Thy Church,
and for all Thy priests,
especially for those who are still wallowing in sins
and blind to the sweet light
of Thy Countenance.
My Jesus,
I give myself as a victim of love to Thee
who gave Thyself as a victim of love for me.
I desire to have no will apart from Thy will,
the perfect expression of Thy Heart's love for me
and for all Thy priests.
I offer myself to Thee also
for all the intentions of the Pope.
I ask Thee to strengthen him and to console him,
and I consecrate him to Thy Mother's
Immaculate Heart.

E IT DONE UNTO ME
according to Thy word.
Lord Jesus, I accept Thy plan.
I give my free and
full consent to Thy will.
I am willing to forsake all else
and leave all else behind.
I am Thy servant and,
by Thy infinite mercy,
the friend of Thy Heart.
Amen.

 MY BELOVED LORD JESUS,
truly present here,
I adore Thee with all the
love of my heart.
It is for this and for no other thing
    that Thou hast brought me here:
to adore Thee, to abide in Thy company,
to seek Thy Face, and to rest upon Thy Heart.
Keep me faithful to the calling Thou hast given me,
and let nothing distract me from Thee,
who art the One Thing Necessary,
and apart from Whom there is nothing in
    heaven or on earth
    to which I will give my heart.
To be near Thee is my happiness.
Hold me in Thy presence,
and let me never depart from the radiance
    of Thy Eucharistic Face.
Amen.

ESUS, JESUS, JESUS,
let nothing take me
out of the radiance
of Thy Eucharistic Face;
rather, let all things work together
to compel me to seek Thy Face
and to adore Thee.

 ES, LORD JESUS,
I consent to lose all save Thee,
for in possessing Thee,
I will lose nothing,
and in loving Thee
I will be loved by Thee,
and in that love find perfect happiness
and the grace to love others
as Thou hast loved me.

ORD JESUS CHRIST,
although I cannot, during this hour,
approach Thee physically
in the Sacrament of Thy love,
I would approach Thee by desire and by faith.
Transport me, I beseech Thee,
by the lifting up of my mind and heart,
to that tabernacle in the world
    where Thou art, at this hour,
most forsaken, utterly forgotten,
and without human company.
Let the radiance of Thy Eucharistic Face
    so penetrate my soul
    that by offering Thee
    adoration and reparation,
even as I am busy doing ordinary things
    in an ordinary way,
I may obtain from Thy Sacred Heart
    the return of at least one priest
    to the Tabernacle
    where Thou waitest for him today.
Amen.

 MY BELOVED JESUS,
I am happy to be in Thy presence.
Thy psalmist said it:
"To be near God is my happiness."
There are no words to describe what it is
    to have Thee—
God from God, Light from Light,
    Very God from Very God—so close.
Thou art hidden, but I see Thee.
Thou art silent, but I hear Thee.
Thou art immobile, but Thou reachest out
    to draw me in and hold me against Thy Heart.

54

One who possesses Thee
  in the Sacrament of Thy love,
possesses everything.
Because Thou art here, I lack nothing.
Because Thou art here, I have nothing to fear.
Because Thou art here, I cannot be lonely.
Because Thou art here, heaven itself is here,
and myriads of angels adoring Thee
  and offering Thee their songs of praise.
Because Thou art here,
I need not search for Thee anywhere else.
Because Thou art here,
my faith possesses Thee,
my hope is anchored to Thee,
my love embraces Thee and will not let Thee go.

ORD JESUS,
Thou askest not the impossible
of me,
  for even when Thou askest what,
to my eyes, appears impossible,
Thou art already making it possible by Thy grace.
To Thee, and to those who love Thee,
nothing is impossible.
I can do all things in Thee
  who strengthenest me to do them.

NITE ME, I BESEECH THEE,
to Thy Eucharistic humility,
to Thy silence, Thy hiddenness,
and Thy ceaseless
prayer to the Father.
Unite me to the uninterrupted oblation
of Thyself to the Father
in the Sacrament of Thy love.
There is no moment in which
Thou art not offering Thyself,
no moment in which
Thy immolation on the Cross
is not re-presented to the Father
from the silence of Thy tabernacles.
Let nothing, then, separate me from Thyself,
the Lamb of God by Whose Blood
the world is redeemed,
souls are washed clean of sin,
and the Father's Heart is moved to pity
for the most hardened sinners
and for the very least of His creatures.
Amen.

 MY BELOVED JESUS,
I adore Thy Eucharistic Face,
the radiance of which is my
unfailing light
in the shadows of this earthly exile.
So long as Thou art with me, I will fear no evil.
Thou art here, close to me,
and I am here, close to Thee,
to believe in Thee, to hope in Thee,
to love Thee, and to adore Thee.
Apart from Thee I desire nothing on earth,
and without Thee, what is heaven?
Here in Thy Eucharistic presence
is heaven on earth.
Here is the joy eternal
of all the angels and blessed.
Here is the fulfilment of the longing in hope
that burns like a fire in the souls of purgatory.

Here is the heart of the Church on earth
  and the glory of the Church in heaven.
Here is the stupendous miracle
  of Thy love for us:
Thy abiding presence as the Lamb who was slain,
and the triumph of Thy Cross and Resurrection.
Why, then, art Thou left alone
  in this Most Holy Sacrament?
Why art Thou forsaken in Thy tabernacles?
Why are Thy churches empty or so rarely visited?
Reveal Thyself again in the Sacrament of Thy love!
Make known Thy presence here
  to those who doubt,
to the ignorant, the indifferent,
and the cold-hearted.
Draw all—baptized and unbaptized—
into the radiance of Thy Eucharistic Face,
and let not a single soul escape the embrace
  of Thy Eucharistic friendship.
Thus wilt Thou satisfy Thine own thirst
  for the faith and love of our souls;
and thus wilt Thou satisfy
  Thine own Heart's longing
  for the love of the hearts
  which Thou hast created for Thyself
  and for no other. *Amen.*

 OME, HOLY GHOST!
Come, living Fire!
Come, Anointing from above!
Come, living Water!
Come, Breath of God!

Mark me with an incision of fire
    for the work to which I have been called.
Sign my soul deeply and indelibly
    for the adoration
    of the Eucharistic Face of the Son,
and for the consolation
    of His Eucharistic Heart.
So burn the mark of this vocation into me
    that I will suffer from every betrayal of it,
and from every infidelity to it.
So seal me for this vocation
    that I will find Thee only in fulfilling it
    and in its perfection
    in the lasting adoration of heaven,
where Thou livest and reignest
    with the Father and the Son.

Let the adoration of the Lamb
    begin for me here on earth today,
and let it increase and deepen in my life
    until it becomes ceaseless:
a spring of joy
    flowing from an inexhaustible source,
Thine own indwelling presence in my soul,
to quench the thirst of the Bridegroom Christ,
and to make fruitful His priesthood in the Church.
Amen.

IVE TO ME, LORD JESUS,
    according to Thy Heart's desire.
    I am an empty vessel waiting
    for Thee to fill me.
I would remain before Thee, silent and empty,
and prepared to be filled
    with whatever it shall please Thee
    to pour into me.
Fill me according to Thy desire,
not only for myself, but for others,
for the souls whom Thou wilt send to me,
that I may give them something pure,
something divine to drink.

CONVERT THOU ME ENTIRELY,
O my beloved Jesus,
   that I may live every moment—
   up to and including
   the very moment of my death—
with my eyes fixed on Thine adorable Face,
and with my heart hidden in Thy piercèd Heart.
Make me, I pray Thee,
   what Thou hast called me to be.
Let me so love Thee and adore Thee
   that I may be for Thine afflicted Heart
   the consoling friend for whom
   Thou hast waited so long.
Leave me not alone, never forsake me,
so that I may never leave Thee alone,
and never forsake Thee.
Fix my vagrant heart before Thy tabernacle—
before the one where Thou art least adored
   and most forgotten—
that I may persevere
   in a watch of adoration, of reparation,
   and of love before Thy Eucharistic Face.
What can I give Thee that Thou hast not given me?
Give Thou, then, to me superabundantly,
so that I may give back to Thee superabundantly.

Give Thou me, I beseech Thee, but a spark
  of Thine own blazing zeal
  for the glory of the Father;
let it consume me entirely as a holocaust
  to the praise of His glory.
Give Thou me, I beseech Thee,
a share in Thy spousal love for the Church,
Thy Bride in heaven and on earth.
Like Thee, with Thee, in Thee,
  let me lay down my life for her.
Give Thou me, I beseech Thee,
Thine own Heart's filial love
  for Thine Immaculate Mother,
that I may love her
  as Thou wouldst have me love her;
that I might serve her with a devotion
  that is true, and pure, and constant.
Give Thou me, I beseech Thee,
the tender compassion with which
  Thou wouldst have me care for souls,
that in my care for them
  they may experience the solicitude
  of Thy Sacred Heart.
Make me, if possible,
more Thy priest today
  than I have ever been before.

Ratify and confirm me in the ineffable grace
    of real participation in the Mystery of the Cross,
where Thou art Priest and Victim.
Burn more deeply into my soul
    the indelible character of Thy priesthood,
and, in that same fire, consume and destroy
    all that dims, obstructs, or impedes
    its glorious radiance,
so that the light of Thy sacrifice
    may shine before men,
and its healing power go forth from me
    as it went forth from Thee,
for Thou, O merciful Saviour,
hast made me Thy priest forever.
A thousand, thousand lifetimes
    would be too little time
    to thank Thee, to bless Thee, to praise Thee
    for so immeasurable a gift.
Give me then, when Thou callest me to Thyself,
an eternity in which to praise Thee beyond the veil
    where, for the moment, Thou art hidden
    in the glory of the Father
    and in the brightness of the Holy Ghost.
Amen.

ILENCE OF THE SACRED HOST,
pervade me.
Hiddenness of the Sacred Host,
envelop me.
Humility of the Sacred Host, shield me.
Poverty of the Sacred Host, be all to me.
Purity of the Sacred Host, cleanse me.
Radiance of the Sacred Host, illumine me.
Countenance hidden in the Sacred Host,
reveal Thyself to me.
Heart all afire in the Sacred Host,
set me ablaze with Thy love.

O Sacred Host, living Flesh and Blood
of the Immolated Lamb,
I adore Thee.

O Sacred Host, living Flesh and Blood
of the Immolated Lamb,
I offer Thee to the Father.

O Sacred Host, living Flesh and Blood
of the Immolated Lamb,
I beseech Thee to unite me to Thyself
now and at the hour of my death. *Amen.*

CPSIA information can be obtained
at www.ICGtesting.com
Printed in the USA
JSHW052128210920
8120JS00001B/28